NEVER BE SAD AGAIN:

The Path to Eternal Happiness.

RYAN LAWSON

COPYRIGHT

TABLE OF CONTENTS

INTRODUCTION

CHAPTER ONE
Know Thy Mind

CHAPTER TWO
Declutter Your Mind & Be Positive

CHAPTER THREE
Handling Difficult Thoughts and Feelings

CHAPTER FOUR
Self Compassion and The Value of Kindness

CHAPTER FIVE
Spreading Happiness

CONCLUSION

INTRODUCTION

Welcome to "Never Be Sad Again: The Path to Eternal Happiness!"

Are you weary of feeling like happiness is playing hide-and-seek with you? Well, it's time to put on your detective hat and embark on an adventure packed with fun, wisdom, and a touch of magic.

In this self-help treasure trove, we'll examine not one, not two, but five delicious paths to unlock the door to eternal bliss. And guess what? You won't need to climb mountains or meditate for hours (unless you want to, of course).

So, get ready to spread happiness like confetti, embrace the superpower of self-compassion, clear your mind from those annoying ideas, handle life's curveballs like a pro, and understand your mind like never before.

Let's swap the frowns for smiles, one excursion at a time. Buckle up and get ready to experience joy like you've never known before! Happiness, here we come! ◉☐‿☐◉

CHAPTER ONE

Know Thy Mind

In our relentless search for contentment, we often overlook the most essential part of our being—the mind. It is within the depths of our minds that the key to true joy lies, waiting to be uncovered. In this chapter, we will embark on a profound exploration of the mind, uncovering its complexities and uncovering the way to lasting happiness. Get ready to embark on a transformative journey of self-discovery as we delve into the profound connection between understanding your mind and finding true joy.

1. The Power of Self-Awareness:
To be aware of one's mind is to understand oneself on the deepest level. Self-awareness is the foundation of personal growth and happiness. Investigate the importance of self-awareness in

unlocking your true potential and achieving genuine happiness. Discover practical techniques to cultivate self-awareness, including mindfulness, introspection, and reflection.

2. The Inner Landscape:
Embark on an intriguing journey into the inner landscape of your mind. Gain insights into the various components of the mind, such as thoughts, emotions, beliefs, and biases. Learn how these elements shape your perception of the world and influence your overall well-being. Uncover the power of thought patterns and beliefs, and how they can either impede or propel you on your path to joy.

3. The Art of Emotional Intelligence:
Emotions are a vital part of the human experience. Develop a deep understanding of your emotions and learn to utilize their transformative power. Explore the concept of emotional intelligence and

its profound impact on your happiness. Discover effective strategies to cultivate emotional intelligence, including emotional awareness, regulation, and empathy.

4. Unraveling the Mind-Body Connection:
The mind and body are intricately interconnected. Gain a deeper appreciation for the mind-body connection and its influence on your overall well-being. Learn how your thoughts and emotions can affect your physical health and vice versa. Explore practices such as meditation, exercise, and stress management techniques that promote harmony between the mind and body.

5. Breaking Free from Limiting Beliefs:
Limiting beliefs can be powerful obstacles on the path to joy. Identify and challenge the limiting beliefs that hold you back from experiencing true happiness. Explore techniques to reframe negative thought patterns and cultivate a positive mindset.

Empower yourself with the tools to let go of self-imposed limitations and embrace the boundless possibilities for joy.

By delving into the depths of your mind, you unlock the door to genuine happiness. Understanding your mind allows you to navigate life's challenges with clarity, resilience, and compassion.

As you embark on this journey of self-discovery, remember that being aware of one's mind is a lifelong pursuit. Embrace the power of self-awareness, cultivate emotional intelligence, nurture a positive outlook, and honor the mind-body connection. In doing so, you will pave the way for lasting joy and embark on a transformative path toward a fulfilling and joyful life.

Take the first step today and embark on the enlightening journey of self-discovery. Be aware of thy mind, and you will find the path to true happiness.

CHAPTER TWO

Declutter Your Mind & Be Positive

What is mind clutter? It's not just the physical mess in your home, it can also build up in our minds. Mental clutter is like a chaotic jumble of thoughts, worries, and distractions that fill up our mental space, leaving us feeling overwhelmed and scattered.

This can include holding onto guilt and regret, being involved in toxic relationships, worrying about the future, not being able to prioritize, having too many commitments, and being overwhelmed by information overload. It's almost like having a hundred computer tabs open at once!

Fortunately, you can declutter your mind just like you can declutter your home. This means managing your thinking patterns to enjoy more peace of mind, presence, clarity, and well-being. By paying attention to your thoughts and reorganizing them, you can create a space for clarity and focus.

Benefits of Decluttering Your Mind

The benefits of decluttering your mind are numerous. You can enjoy enhanced mental clarity, reduced stress and anxiety, improved productivity, heightened emotional well-being, increased self-awareness, enhanced focus and concentration, and improved sleep quality.

If you want to declutter your mind, there are multiple ways to find mental peace. Consider which practices will best address your mental clutter and practice them every day. With a little effort, you can enjoy a more mindful and conscious way of life.

1. Focused Deep Breathing

When we're feeling overwhelmed, anxious, or stressed, our breathing often changes. We may start to breathe rapidly or feel short of breath. But by simply paying attention to our breathing and posture, we can create a calmer state of mind and body.

One of the best ways to take control of our thoughts is to practice slow, deep, rhythmic breathing. This type of breathing stimulates the parasympathetic nervous system, which helps to reduce our heart rate, relax our muscles, and normalize brain function.

2. Learn Meditation

Don't let the stereotypes of meditating cave dwellers put you off from trying it out. Meditation has many benefits, such as helping to control worry and overthinking and providing a host of health benefits. The key to finding satisfaction with meditation is to practice it daily.

3. Reframing Negative Thoughts

We all have negative thoughts, but we don't have to be victims of them. We can recognize this tendency and change it by building the reframing habit. The first step is to notice our thought patterns and interrupt them before they get out of control. We can do this by becoming the "watcher" of our thoughts without attaching to them or judging them.

We can also interrupt our negative thoughts by saying "Stop!" out loud and visualizing a heavy metal door slamming on them. Then, we can distract ourselves with something that will occupy our minds.

4. Teach Your Old Mind New Tricks

We can't overcome millions of years of evolutionary wiring through sheer willpower, but we can manage the pain by being more proactive in what we allow to remain in our thoughts.

We can interrupt cluttered thinking and disassociate from negative thoughts by challenging a negative thought and replacing it with a more positive one, practicing acceptance rather than struggling against reality, taking mindful action that focuses on our values, goals, or priorities, and setting a worry timer.

5. Identify Your Core Values

It can be difficult to figure out what's truly important and differentiate those things from the obligations that seem important at first. Taking the time to examine our obligations can help us to identify our core values and prioritize them.

If you're like most people, it can be hard to manage the sheer amount of information we're exposed to daily. We have more access to data and possessions than ever before, but no instructions on how to handle it all. This can lead to feeling overwhelmed and not knowing how to prioritize.

Fortunately, there is a simple solution to cutting through the noise of modern life and making effective decisions: define your core values. Your core values can be a measuring stick for all of your choices and decisions, helping you stay focused on the person you want to be and the life you want to lead.

6. Clarify Your Life Priorities

Once you're done with your core values, use the information to further clarify your life priorities, and ask yourself how you want to spend your time, energy, and money. Without knowing our priorities, we can easily be swayed by the pressures of life. To help you establish your priorities, consider the seven main life areas:

- ☐ Career

- ☐ Family
- ☐ Marriage/love partnership
- ☐ Spiritual/personal growth/self-improvement
- ☐ Leisure/Social
- ☐ Life management (i.e. home tasks, financial planning, budgeting, etc.)
- ☐ Health and fitness.

If you sleep 8 hours a day, that leaves 16 waking hours. Deducting 2 hours for personal hygiene and eating leaves 14 waking hours a day or 98 hours a week. To make it easier, let's round that up to 100 hours a week. How would you prioritize those seven key areas of your life? How many hours of those 100 per week would you prefer to devote to each area (using your values to help guide you)?

To help you find your priorities, answer two simple questions:

1) How different from your ideal is the reality of your present life priorities?

2) What steps must you take in order to concentrate your attention on the things that are most important to you?

Start with the priority that can make the most positive difference in your life or where you feel the most imbalance.

7. Be More Present In Your Relationships
Another source of mental clutter can be relationship problems. To be more present in your relationships, practice empathic listening and mindful speaking. Empathic listening is a willingness to listen to the other person's words in a non-judgmental way. Ask open-ended questions and reflect to the speaker what you heard them say. When it comes to mindful speaking, pay close attention to what you say during a conversation, particularly in your love relationship.

Place a mental barrier between your thoughts and words, understanding the power your words have on the most important people in your life. Instead of just reacting to someone's words or actions, take a moment to choose your words wisely. Speak in a way that is loving, compassionate, and respectful, and try to use a calm, non-threatening voice, even if the other person is agitated or angry.

One way to do this is to practice loving-kindness meditation. This type of meditation focuses on developing feelings of warmth towards others. It can help you reduce negative thinking about them and improve your relationships. It also cultivates your awareness of others as human beings deserving of compassion and love, even when they are being difficult, which can reduce conflicts and improve your well-being.

8. Simply Your Activities

Another way to reduce stress and mental clutter is to simplify your activities. We often get caught up in the treadmill of tasks and obligations, leaving little time for things that allow us to be present and fully engaged.

It's hard to break free from the busyness trap, but cutting back and expunging non-essential activities can help. Start by embracing it as a worthy endeavor and acknowledging that busyness is contributing to your mental clutter. Prioritize your daily activities by focusing on your core values, purge your commitments and obligations, focus on three main daily goals, and allow for time to relax and do nothing.

9. Practice Gratitude
Developing a gratitude practice is also beneficial. Our minds have a habit of focusing on negative events, but we can counteract this by training ourselves to focus on the positive. Make it a habit

to stop for a moment throughout your day to reflect on all you are grateful for. Consider what your life would be like without the person or thing you are grateful for to spark the emotions of gratitude.

10. Use Affirmations

Practice using affirmations. These are positive statements you repeat to challenge negative and self-destructive thinking patterns. Pay attention to the current theme of your negative thoughts and use affirmations to replace them with positive ones.

Negative thoughts can be hard to shake off, but it's important to replace them with positive affirmations. For example, if you feel like no one cares about you, you could tell yourself, "I am a kind, lovable, and desirable person who easily attracts people who care about me and treat me well." It's important to create affirmations that you believe can become true for you. If you don't feel like you're lovable, you could say, "Every day, I am becoming more of the person I want to be who attracts the type of people I want in my life."

To help make positive thinking a habit, keep a list of affirmations with you and practice speaking them aloud to yourself in front of a mirror. You can also use them as prompts for journaling or meditation. The more you practice, the more you'll get used to thinking positively about your life.

11. Spend Time In Nature
Another great way to declutter your mind is to spend time in nature. Shinrin-yoku, or "forest bathing", is a Japanese practice that involves immersing yourself in the sights, sounds, smells, and emotions of the natural world.

Just 10-20 minutes of nature cleansing time can lower your blood pressure, heart rate, and stress levels. To get the most out of your natural experience, leave your distractions behind and pay attention to your senses.

12. Jot down Thoughts and Feelings
Writing down your thoughts and feelings in a journal can also be incredibly helpful in clearing your mind. Brain dump all of your worries, frustrations, ideas, and feelings into your journal and you'll be able to gain a clearer perspective on the situation.

13. Making a to-do list and prioritizing tasks can also help to reduce stress. Write down all the tasks that need to be done in order of priority and focus on completing each task one at a time.

14. Make a Designated Space for Relaxation
Creating a designated space for relaxation can also be beneficial. This doesn't have to be an entire room, but could just be a corner of a room or a comfortable chair in your bedroom. Make sure this

space is kept clutter-free and peaceful, with minimal distractions.

15. Limit Your Time On Social Media

Limit your exposure to social media and news to reduce information overload. Taking a digital sabbatical for one day a week or unplugging for a few hours each day can make a huge difference in finding inner peace.

16. Engage in Regular Physical Exercise

Engaging in regular physical exercise is a great way to keep your body healthy and your mind stress-free. Exercise releases endorphins which can help to improve our moods, and it also helps to create a sense of focus and purpose.

17. Try Delegating Tasks

If you're feeling overwhelmed by all the tasks you need to do, try delegating them to lighten your mental load. Remember that you don't have to take on the responsibility of everything for the entire family. Delegating tasks can help you realize that some of the things causing mental clutter aren't actually your responsibility.

18. Set clear boundaries
It's also important to set clear boundaries with others to protect your mental space. This could mean saying no to something that doesn't fit within your timeline or values or setting firm guidelines around communication. Establishing healthy boundaries will create a sense of security and respect, and help to keep your mental space free from any unwanted negativity.

19. Practicing forgiveness towards yourself and others is another great way to reduce mental clutter. Letting go of any guilt or regrets from the past will help to create a sense of peace within.

20. Take Regular Breaks to Rest

Taking regular breaks to rest and recharge is also essential for good mental health. Breaks give us time to relax and clear our minds, and they can help to reduce stress levels and improve concentration and focus.

21. Engage in Hobbies or Activities that Give you Joy

Engaging in hobbies or activities that bring you joy and relaxation is also important. Not only do they help to relax and clear the mind, but they also help to build a sense of purpose and satisfaction in life.

22. Have a Consistent Sleep Routine

Establishing a consistent sleep routine is also key for keeping our minds clear and focused. Aim for 7-9 hours of quality rest each night, and try to put away all devices one to two hours before going to bed.

23. Practice Self-Care Activities

Taking regular time out to pamper yourself, relax, and do the things you love is a great way to clear your mind of any unnecessary thoughts. Schedule time in advance so you don't get too caught up with work or other responsibilities, and make sure that each day has some kind of self-care activity scheduled. Even if it's just 5 minutes of self-care, it can make a big difference.

24. Clear out your physical space to create a sense of order and peace

Having a cluttered physical space can be a reflection of mental clutter, so it's important to take the time to tidy up and organize your environment. Whether it's at home or work, decluttering your space can help to create a sense of order and peace.

25. Learn to say "no" to things that don't fit with your priorities and values

It can be hard to say no, but it's essential for reducing mental distraction. Think about what tasks and commitments are important to you, and then just say no to the things that don't align with your life priorities and values. It may be difficult, but it's the best thing you can do for yourself and your mental health.

26. Limit multitasking and focus on one task at a time

Multitasking doesn't really exist. Our brains can only really focus on one thing at a time, so trying to do two or more things at once is actually slowing us down. Try to limit multitasking to reduce the amount of mental interruption and clutter in your mind. Instead of doing three things at once, focus on just one task until it's complete before moving on to the next.

27. Surround yourself with positive and supportive people

The people in our lives can have a huge impact on the way we think, so it's important to make sure we're surrounding ourselves with positive, supportive, and encouraging people. Having these positive relationships around us helps to reduce mental clutter and stress. Take a look at who you spend your time with - do they bring out the best in you and lift you? Toxic relationships can create feelings of self-doubt, guilt, and anxiety - so it's important to identify these relationships, practice healthy boundaries, and learn how to let them go.

28. Let go of perfectionism and accept imperfections

There's no such thing as perfect. Perfect is imperfect. Perfectionism can lead to a lot of stress because it's impossible to be perfect. It's important to practice letting go of the need for perfection and accepting imperfections. Be kinder and more compassionate towards yourself, and let go of any expectations that don't positively serve you.

Remember that you're human and that there will be times when things don't go according to plan.

Being Positive

Being positive is all about having an optimistic outlook on life and being grateful for what you have. It's not about never feeling negative emotions or struggling with pessimistic thoughts. Everyone has days when they feel down or discouraged, but positive thinkers don't let their negative emotions control them. Instead, they focus on finding solutions and try to look on the bright side of life.

How To Be More Positive

If you want to be more positive, there are a few things you can do.

1. Gratitude

Practicing gratitude is a great way to start. Make a list of things you're grateful for and write them down in a gratitude journal. It could be something as simple as a beautiful, sunny day or your cat nuzzling against your hand. Focusing on the good things in your life will help you shift into a more positive frame of mind.

2. Savor Anticipation
Another way to be more positive is to savor the anticipation. Find something to look forward to each day and research has found that it can help improve your mood and reduce stress.

Finding something to look forward to each day can help you stay positive, even when things don't go your way. Whether it's visiting your favorite bookstore, grabbing coffee with friends, taking a stroll in the park, or reading a book, make sure to make time for something that brings you joy.

3. Practice Mindfulness

Practicing mindfulness is a great way to stay in the present moment and become more aware of your thoughts and feelings. When you're feeling overwhelmed, take a few deep breaths and focus on your body and the sounds around you. This can help you identify and replace negative thoughts with more positive ones.

4. Smile

Smiling can also help you feel better, even if you don't feel like it. Smiling releases chemicals in your brain that make you feel happy and relaxed. Plus, it can help you view the world from a more positive perspective.

5. Use Positive Self-Talk

Positive self-talk is also important. The things you say to yourself can influence how you think and feel, so it's important to be kind to yourself.

Replace negative self-talk with positive affirmations and you'll start to feel more optimistic.

Positive people tend to be optimistic, grateful, helpful, compassionate, happy, upbeat, and humorous. On the other hand, negative people are usually pessimistic, ungrateful, ruminate on problems, unhelpful, apathetic, unhappy, cynical, and serious.

Benefits of Being Positive

Being positive has many benefits, both mentally and physically. It can help improve your mental well-being, increase your happiness, and lead to better physical health. It can also help you build stronger relationships and be more motivated to achieve your goals.

However, it's important to be aware of the potential pitfalls of being less positive. Negative thoughts can lead to depression and anxiety, and it can be difficult to take care of yourself physically. It can also negatively impact relationships and make it hard to feel motivated. Finally, negativity can be contagious, so it's important to be mindful of the people you surround yourself with.

Can You Be Too Positive?

If you're always trying to be positive and deny the presence of negative emotions, it could be a sign that you're being too positive. This is known as toxic positivity and it can make people feel unsupported and ashamed when they're dealing with difficult times or darker emotions.

Being positive has many advantages, like increased happiness, better relationships, and more success in life. But there are also some potential drawbacks, such as depression and anxiety, negative physical health effects, and difficulty maintaining healthy relationships. To be more positive, hang out with positive people, do things that make you feel good, and practice self-care.

CHAPTER THREE

Handling Difficult Thoughts and Emotions

In today's world, life is often hectic and filled with family, relationships, and work-related stressors. This, combined with the pressures of technology and society, can have a negative impact on marriages. Consequently, it is not uncommon for couples to experience a range of difficult emotions such as anger, confusion, fear, loneliness, and sadness. These emotions can be some of the most powerful forces in a person's life.

In this chapter, we will discuss some effective strategies to manage and respond to challenging thoughts and emotions before they become too overwhelming. It is important to remember that difficult times come with difficult thoughts and emotions, and this is a normal part of life. If you find that these feelings are interfering with your enjoyment of life for two weeks or more, it is important to seek help from a doctor.

In addition, some strategies can help reduce the impact of these feelings and help you become more emotionally resilient. It is important to understand that thoughts and emotions are neither good nor bad, and it is more useful to see them as either difficult or pleasant. Don't be too quick to judge them; instead, try to understand why these thoughts and feelings are coming up and how they make you feel.

When we are stressed or have something upsetting happen, we may experience a 'racing mind' and the same unpleasant thoughts occurring over and over again. This can lead to unpleasant emotions such as excessive worry, shame, and even despair. To sort out helpful and unhelpful thoughts and respond accordingly, it is important to be aware of the types of thoughts that can be harmful. Examples of unhelpful thoughts include those that put you or others down, conjure worst-case scenarios, compare your situation to others, or remind you of how things 'should' be.

To develop more awareness of your thoughts, it can be beneficial to question them.

Mentally ask yourself questions like:

- Are these ideas accurate?
- Is there proof that what I'm concerned about is a legitimate concern?
- Is there a valid justification for these thoughts?
- Has my imagination got the better of me?
- What's the worst thing that might happen?
- What's another way I might look at this problem?
- Are they assumptions I have made that are incorrect?

By challenging your ideas you may be able to diminish their influence over you. Sometimes the support of a counselor or therapist may help you create better mental habits in this manner. And in the same line, cultivating greater attentive awareness (purposely being aware of what you're feeling in the present without judgment) is tremendously beneficial in coping with negative ideas.

Feeling and Identifying our Emotions

Similarly, most of us seldom, if ever, consciously tune into how our emotions feel in terms of sensations in the body. The only time you tend to notice how your body feels is if you're in pain or you feel poorly, or feelings that accompany being overly hot or cold or hungry for example.

Most of the time we don't even consciously recognize the body sensations that accompany hunger, thirst, wanting to go to the bathroom, or an itch that we need to scratch. We just take action without spending a second recognizing what the feelings were that drove us to act on them.

It might be shocking to understand that emotions are, in fact, feelings in our bodies. As most of us don't pay much mind to these experiences, we tend to think they happen in our thoughts. Tuning in and recognizing sensations and feelings is a simple but effective method to control your emotions. We're often tempted to "fudge over" or avoid experiencing challenging feelings and emotions.

There is strong evidence from a variety of studies that demonstrate when we actively identify and put into words what we're experiencing, we can relax our 'stress response' - the portion of our nervous system that is active when we're anxious – and allow ourselves to better control our emotions. In other words, if we don't allow our emotions to be there, if we ignore them, they're going to affect us much more.

So, when you're experiencing tough emotions, it may be really useful to consciously tune into your body and your senses and identify what you are feeling. It takes practice, and the more regularly you do it the simpler it gets.

Again, one effective method to build this habit of mind is to practice mindfulness or other types of meditation. Having a more stable mood and being able to better control emotions is widely stated by those who practice mindfulness, various types of meditation, and movement-oriented disciplines such as yoga, Tai Chi, and other martial arts. These techniques may assist to create better awareness of sensations and emotions.

You are not your ideas or emotions

It may be quite beneficial to remind yourself that you are not your thoughts and emotions. Thoughts and sentiments come and go and alter all the time. Watching them rise and fade away, almost as if you are watching a storm pass by, might help you feel less overwhelmed when they're very tough.

When you are articulating how you feel, it might be good to adopt less personal language. For example, rather than using "I am so stressed" you may say "I feel so stressed" or replace "I am so overwhelmed" with "I feel so overwhelmed". In this manner, you may remove yourself from what you are experiencing so that it doesn't define you.

One extremely significant approach to overcoming these challenging feelings is mindfulness! Practicing mindfulness assists you to calm down and comfort yourself. In this mood, you have room to consider and deliberately reply, rather than react.

Following these six stages will allow you to understand and cope with your challenging emotions thoughtfully:

How to Deal With Tough Emotions

Dealing with tough emotions can be a challenge, but with a few conscious actions, you can learn to handle them healthily.

1. Turn towards your feelings with acceptance. When you become aware of the emotion you are feeling, take a moment to note where it is in your body. You may experience it as a stomachache, a constriction of your throat, the hammering of your heart, or tension somewhere. Don't ignore it or

push it aside. Instead, sit with it and listen to what it is trying to teach you.

2. Identify and label the emotion. Instead of stating, "I am angry", say, "This is anger" or, "This is anxiety." This helps you to recognize its presence, while simultaneously allowing you to remain detached from it.

3. Accept your emotions. Don't deny the feelings you are feeling. Acknowledge and accept it, and then give kindness and compassion towards yourself.

4. Realize the impermanence of your feelings. Every emotion is fleeting. Allow yourself to see and observe it with patience, giving it the liberty to transform and eventually fade.

5. Inquire and investigate. After you have calmed yourself, take a moment to explore what happened.

Ask yourself what prompted you, what is leading you to feel this way, and what discomfort you're experiencing. Consider what was said or done and compare it to your values.

What were your expectations of the situation? What reactions or judgments made you furious or anxious? Is this something that keeps happening? Asking yourself these questions and looking into the origins of your tough feelings might help you gain understanding and empathy for what you are going through.

Rather than going on autopilot, trust your innermost, authentic self to answer these questions about the circumstance. This will offer you a different outlook and allow both you and your partner to be more present and connected.

6. Let go of the need to control your emotions. The key to regulating your emotions thoughtfully is to

let go of the impulse to control them. Instead, be open to the outcome and what happens. Listen to your partner and genuinely hear what they are feeling. This is the only way to develop a profound grasp of your emotions and the dynamics inside your relationship.

Mindfully dealing with emotions is challenging and it takes time. Be gentle, sympathetic, and patient with yourself and your relationship. You are in this together!

We are lucky to live in a world where you and your spouse can take the time to investigate, discuss, and learn about mindfulness and your emotions. Don't take anything for granted, for life is precious and transient.

CHAPTER FOUR

Self Compassion and the Value of Kindness

Most people conceive of self-compassion as being kind to themselves. Although that is an element of the term, self-compassion encompasses a method of responding to oneself in a way that helps you to become more emotionally flexible, able to negotiate hard emotions and increase your connection to self and others. The capacity to relate to oneself in a caring way may sound straightforward enough but it may be quite a problem.

You may find it simple to be empathetic toward a friend or loved one when they come to you with a personal difficulty or a hard scenario. Your answer to them may be one of understanding, hope, direction, and encouragement.

However, when we are faced with our issues, we tend to be a little more harsh or judgmental with ourselves. We scrutinize our thoughts and activities in a way that might leave us feeling worthless, humiliated, and dissatisfied with ourselves. To keep going forward, we may urge ourselves to "buck up," or "get over it." Although the purpose is to assist move us ahead during times of emotional struggle, this style of connecting to oneself may produce an enormous amount of tension and become a huge hurdle in our capacity to feel happiness inside ourselves and with others.

Elements of Self-Compassion

Dr. Kristin Neff, a psychologist and pioneering researcher on the subject of self-compassion, defines three characteristics of self-compassion:

Self-Kindness: When persons who practice self-compassion find themselves in hard situations, they know that being flawed or falling short at times is a part of living. The capacity to handle these events without putting oneself down is an element of self-compassion.

Common Humanity: When we are faced with hardships, it can be easy to feel alone in our experience, as if others would not be able to connect to what we are going through. People who practice self-compassion recognize that some of these obstacles are part of the shared human experience.

Mindfulness: Practicing self-compassion entails being able to recognize our painful feelings without exaggerating them or disregarding them. This thoughtful and balanced position allows us to not become emotionally reactive.

How to Practice Self-Compassion

There are a range of activities that might help us learn the practice of self-compassion:

1. Imagine how you would talk to a buddy.
We may frequently give pleasant words, hope, and encouragement to friends or loved ones. When going through a tough period, take a minute to ponder how you might behave to a close friend if they were going through a similar circumstance.

2. Become an observer.
During moments when we are challenged or struggling emotionally, it might feel like we are merely responding and trying to emotionally survive the present. By slowing down, we may take a short step back to observe our experience. Looking at the wider view can help us keep things in perspective and help us see critical information that may have been overlooked otherwise.

3. Change your self-talk.

Notice how you talk to yourself in instances when you are experiencing unpleasant emotions. Work to reinterpret your critical self-statements in a more positive, caring approach. This new tone may sound more like a mentor or champion, rather than a critic or judge.

4. Keep a journal and write it out.

Take time each day to write up some of the issues you are encountering. Note occasions as your thoughts tend to wander into critical words or you begin to feel alone in your experiences. As you would with self-talk, consciously recast any critical words with a softer, more empathetic tone to explore if it could feel different.

5. Become clear about what you desire.

As you practice techniques to reframe critical ideas into more loving self-talk, you might start finding signs as to what you are needing and desire. Take time to examine what you want, need, or crave in your life. Clarifying these demands can help you focus on where you want to go and what you are working for, helping to enhance motivation and happiness.

6. Care for yourself.
Sometimes we take care of others and forget, or simply disregard, the need to take care of ourselves. When practicing self-compassion you understand that you have needs to be addressed as well and are deserving of engaging in those self-care practices.

The capacity to build self-care habits might assist minimize the temptation to engage in harmful coping behaviors when faced with obstacles and stress.

The Effect of Self-Compassion on Your Emotions

As a discipline, self-compassion can be effective in controlling your emotions.

Helps to Calm Negative Emotions
The practice of self-compassion—compassionate thought in particular—has been demonstrated to create positive psychological modifications of unpleasant feelings. Using self-compassion practices can assist in reducing the sensation of negative emotion and allow people to recall that they are not alone in their experiences of anguish, grief, and loss.

In the practice of compassionate remarks and reappraisal, the sense of unpleasant emotion can feel soothed, allowing a way for focused observation and good decision-making.

Practicing self-compassion can also allow for the emergence of creativity and motivation.

Helps to Increase Positive Emotions
Self-compassion has been proven to create good emotion, notably calming, warm, and safe sensations. Although this may surely aid in times of hardship, it can also be useful in our regular life practices.

We face everyday contacts in our personal life, at work, or even with strangers, that have the potential to elicit a reflexive emotional reaction. Using practices of self-compassion can assist us to become more attentive to ourselves and our decision-making, resulting in more balanced and beneficial relationships with others.

The practice of self-compassion might be completely different from anything you have done previously. Although the approaches are designed to help us relate better to ourselves and better navigate hard emotional events, it may feel a bit unpleasant when you begin to use some of these ways. Be patient with yourself and realize that we cannot control every element of our life, including how soon we can turn old, self-critical behaviors into new, healthy, and compassionate habits.

Pursuing happiness via the practice of self-compassion is a gift to yourself and the people around you. In practicing self-compassion, you may notice that relationships with others soften and become less reactive, you may find yourself willing to go forward in an area where you previously felt a bit stuck. You may begin experiencing happiness as you search out new, healthier ways of living and relating to yourself.

The Value of Kindness

In our pursuit of happiness, we frequently miss the immense influence that simple acts of kindness can have on our wellness. Kindness may be life-changing, not only for those on the receiving end but also for the giver.

What Does Kindness Mean?

The dictionary definition of kindness is one thing, and we all know it when we see it, but is that all there is to it? We believe there is more to kindness than what it looks like or how it is characterized.

What Does Kindness Look Like?

When people question, "What is the meaning of kindness?" There are a few ways to answer. The most evident is the definition of compassion. Merriam-Webster defines kindness as the quality or state of being nice. Some kind synonyms and similar words are benevolence, grace, and civility.

But let's take a deeper look. Kindness can take many forms. It might be a kind act, a nice deed, or compassion, but it can also be helping someone avoid a mistake through concern or harsh love. Sometimes, people need to work through their problems to evolve, and in that instance, it would be kind to step back and trust them to manage it. Kindness is about helping people in ways that work for them, not about how it makes you appear.

The Ripple Effect of Kindness

The ripple effect of being nice is a significant phenomenon that reveals the far-reaching impacts of our actions. When we choose to behave with kindness towards others, it sets off a cascade of positive effects that extend beyond the initial act itself. Here's how it works:

1. Direct Recipient: The initial ripple is experienced by the person directly on the receiving

end of our compassion. Whether it's a kind word, a helping hand, or a thoughtful gesture, it can provide joy, bring a smile to their face, and provide a sense of support or comfort. They may be inspired by our kindness and be more willing to carry it on to others.

2. Inspired Observers: Kindness is contagious. When people observe acts of kindness, they are generally motivated and elevated by the positive display of empathy and compassion. Observing acts of kindness can restore their trust in mankind, remind them of the goodness in people, and inspire them to engage in their acts of compassion.

3. Reciprocation: The wave of compassion spreads beyond the first deed and might lead to a reciprocal response. The individual who received kindness may feel inspired to pay it forward and exhibit generosity to someone else. They may be compelled to extend a helping hand, offer a word of

encouragement, or do an act of kindness in their unique way.

4. Community and Connection: As more individuals engage in acts of kindness, a sense of community and connection is established. Kindness can break down barriers, develop trust, and improve relationships. It fosters an environment where people feel supported, appreciated, and connected.

5. Ripple Continues: The ripple effect of kindness does not stop with a single act or within a particular community. It continues to spread, touching the lives of more and more individuals. Each act of kindness can inspire numerous acts of compassion, generating an exponential impact. It creates a wave that stretches far beyond our direct grasp, influencing individuals, families, neighborhoods, and even entire societies.

Compassion and Happiness

What brings us joy? How does being compassionate boost our happiness? We often consider this topic and hunt for the answer. You could feel joyful when you are listening to music that you truly appreciate or watching a movie that brings back wonderful memories or even just spending some time outdoors. But happiness can also come from being sympathetic and nice to one another. Research has told us again and time again that compassion and empathy are the cornerstone of our pleasure.

It is recognized that helping others and spreading compassion can not only bring joy to people around us but can also bring us joy. Being compassionate is more than just being kind, it is the deliberation behind each deed that gives it purpose and force.

Compassion Can Take Many Forms

Being empathetic to others could be displayed in numerous ways. This could be through monetary gifts to your local charity, or through your time. Dedicating your time to supporting the causes you are passionate about and helping people in need can enhance your mood and raise your happiness as you can feel the good results of your activities. The individual who receives your act of kindness will likewise feel a similar increase in happiness!

Another approach to practicing compassion is simply listening. At times, life can seem overwhelming. Problems emerge, worries and anxiety occupy our minds and this can have a bad impact on our mood and mental well-being. Therefore, by simply being present for the people around you, you can help to relieve their load. The consequence is a joyful state of being while releasing some stress for another. Both of you will feel empowered and a bit lighter. This action may be reciprocated towards you when you need it or passed through to someone else. That is how giving works and compassion is developed and shared.

Showing compassion for yourself will help you be happier too! Practicing self-compassion is an important form of compassion that many should indulge in.

As you practice self-compassion, you learn to be kind to yourself, listen to your body and mind, and recognize what you may need to do to take care of yourself. This will allow you to prioritize your mental, physical, and emotional well-being. So take the time to make sure that you are eating well, exercising, and getting enough rest and sleep, as this may help restore balance to your life and make you happier too!

Giving Is A Way To Show Compassion To Others And Yourself

Being a compassionate person not only makes the people who receive it happy, but it may make you happy too! Compassion allows us to develop stronger connections with one another, creating a strong sense of belonging. This sensation of belonging can make us feel wanted, loved, and needed, which in turn, makes us feel happy with the lives we lead. These are just a few instances of how you might exercise compassion within your community, to those around you, and for yourself.

Showing Compassion

There are a lot of ways to express and demonstrate compassion to others. Speak with kindness, apologize when you have made a mistake, listen attentively and without prejudice, cheer on others, offer to help someone with a task, be pleased for someone else's success, accept people for who they are, forgive people for their errors, show respect, express gratitude and appreciation, be patient.

When you practice compassion, you start by comprehending another person's position. You look at what they are going through without judgment and try to envision how you would feel in their place. Compassion and empathy have comparable features, but compassion goes a step further. Instead of just seeing yourself in their position, compassion inspires you to take action to support that individual. Because you can experience those emotions so intensely—almost as if it is happening to you—there is a tremendous impulse to find a method to modify the situation or minimize the other person's pain.

Kindness is a great gift that can improve lives, bring delight to others, and preserve our happiness. By recognizing kindness as a core value, we access a stream of compassion and empathy within ourselves. Let compassion drive your actions, for in doing so, you enter a path to immense joy and a life enriched by meaningful connections. Embrace the value of kindness, develop it inside yourself, and produce a wave of positivity that overcomes boundaries, spreads joy, and leads to contentment.

CHAPTER FIVE

Spreading Happiness

The literal meaning of spreading happiness is to make people feel pleased. This can be done by making them laugh or smile, but there are other ways to do this as well! It is necessary to choose hobbies that you enjoy doing, such as studying or playing sports, but it is just as important to be among others who are pleasant. The greatest way to do this is by being around other optimistic people. They tend to bring out the best in you and choose to be joyful.

Spreading happiness is a powerful and important effort that can improve lives and generate a positive ripple effect in our communities. Here are some simple ways to promote happiness in everyday life:

1. Be gentle to yourself! You need to experience compassion towards yourself first since it will be impossible to distribute kindness if you do not know what it is. When you engage in activities that you love, such as singing, art, dancing, cooking, or being around the people you love, it becomes simpler to spread kindness to those around you. When you enjoy the wonderful gestures and be kind to yourself, you can radiate happiness.

2. Share a smile. Sharing a grin with friends or even strangers might help brighten up their day. This is the ideal approach to spreading happiness, as there is always a reason to make you grin. Remember that when you smile, the whole world smiles with you.

3. Give compliments. Everyone enjoys compliments, especially when they are directed to something they put a lot of effort into. If you notice someone doing something fantastic, tell

them. Compliments go a long way in spreading happiness.

4. Engage in chats and laughs. We tend to get caught up in the bustle of the day and our hectic schedules, so it is necessary to take a step back and communicate. Engaging in discussion with individuals around, especially those who may seem sad, and making them laugh will lighten up their day.

5. Be nice and thankful to everyone. Being nice is rewarding and takes nothing from you. Everyone loves to feel appreciated and needed, so thank people for even the tiny things they do.

6. Do something good for others. In a study from Oxford University, there is a benefit that cooking and baking have on your happiness when you do it. People that routinely eat meals with others tend to feel happier. A home-cooked dinner has a special

impact of spreading happiness from the aroma it emits and leaves everyone feeling well taken care of, so gather the gang together, cook them something that will nourish the body and the soul, and pass on the love.

7. Listening with intention. Showing someone that you are listening to them with your entire attention is a simple method to make them feel valued. Providing some helpful counsel can have a good impact on their day. Showing your support through body language, such as nodding in agreement, may be a terrific way to offer your encouragement and spread joy.

8. Leading by example. This is an efficient way to boost happiness. Showing others your positive attitude, generosity, and joy can be encouraging. To do this, seek to be a role model by living with integrity and displaying compassion and gratitude. Additionally, share your enjoyment with

excitement and charity, and celebrate the triumphs of others.

Furthermore, motivate people to find their happiness by sharing your experiences and thoughts. Encourage them to pursue their passions and retain a positive mindset. By following these steps, we may create a ripple effect of joy and well-being in our lives and communities. Every simple act of kindness and every positive connection can add to our collective movement.

CONCLUSION

As we wrap up "Never Be Sad Again: The Path To Eternal Happiness," we look back on the incredible journey we've been on. This book has been a shining beacon, guiding us to a life of bliss, purpose, and unyielding positivity. Through its five chapters, we've explored the depths of the mind, embraced self-compassion and kindness, and discovered practical strategies to handle difficult thoughts and feelings. Now, with our newfound knowledge and tools, we are ready to spread cheer to the world!

In Chapter 1, "Know Thy Mind," we uncovered the might of self-awareness and understanding our minds. By delving into the complexities of our thoughts, emotions, and beliefs, we gained remarkable insights into the factors that shape our happiness. Acknowledging the importance of self-awareness, we now have a strong base to build our path to lasting joy.

Chapter 2, "Declutter Your Mind & Be Positive," gave us the power to let go of negativity and cultivate a positive mindset. Through the practice of decluttering our minds, we released the weight of pessimism and welcomed the endless possibilities that lie ahead. By focusing on gratitude, adopting optimistic thinking, and nurturing a positive outlook, we rewired our minds for happiness.

In Chapter 3, "Handling Difficult Thoughts and Feelings," we faced the challenges that come with our journey toward happiness. We discovered effective strategies to manage difficult thoughts and emotions, building resilience and empowering ourselves to overcome obstacles. By recognizing and accepting our feelings, we found the strength to rise above them, forging a path toward inner peace and contentment.

Chapter 4, "Self Compassion and The Value of Kindness," taught us the importance of extending compassion not only to others but also to ourselves. By embracing self-compassion, we fostered a deep sense of acceptance, love, and forgiveness. At the same time, we realized the tremendous impact that acts of kindness have on our happiness and the well-being of others. Through these powerful practices, we cultivated a sense of interconnectedness and found fulfillment in nurturing and supporting those around us.

Finally, in Chapter 5, "Spreading Happiness," we took our newfound knowledge and shared it with the world. By becoming beacons of positivity and kindness, we created a ripple effect that spread far beyond our immediate circles. Through our actions, we became catalysts for change, inspiring others to embark on their journeys toward happiness. In so doing we created a brighter and more harmonious world for all.

As we finish this transformative journey, remember that the path to happiness is not without its challenges. It requires continuous effort, self-reflection, and a commitment to nurturing our well-being. But armed with the wisdom gained from these five chapters, we have the tools and mindset to tackle any obstacles that may come our way. We have discovered that happiness is not a destination but a way of life—a choice we make each day to embrace joy, cultivate kindness, and spread love.